WITHDRAWN

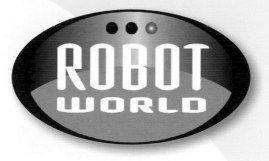

Robots
for Work
and Fun

by Steve Parker

amicus

Published by Amicus
P.O. Box 1329
Mankato, MN 56002

Printed in the United States of America, at
Corporate Graphics in North Mankato, Minnesota.

Library of Congress Cataloging-in-Publication Data
Parker, Steve, 1952-
    Robots for work and fun / by Steve Parker.
        p. cm. – (Robot world)
    Includes index.
    Summary: "Discusses how robots are used for
recreation and work. Also discusses advances in
robotics, and how we benefit from the jobs these
robots do"–Provided by publisher.
    ISBN 978-1-60753-071-8 (library binding)
    1. Robots, Industrial–Juvenile literature. 2.
Mechanical toys–Juvenile literature. I. Title.
    TJ211.2.P355 2011
    629.8'92–dc22

                                    2010001127

Created by Appleseed Editions Ltd.
Designed by Guy Callaby
Edited by Mary-Jane Wilkins
Picture research by Su Alexander

Picture acknowledgements
Title page Stephen Hird/Reuters/Corbis; 4 Car Culture/Corbis;
5 Randy Faris/Corbis; 6 Peter Ginter/Science Faction/Corbis;
7 Bettmann/Corbis; 8 Vario Images GmbH & Co.KG/Alamy;
9t Pascal Goetgheluck/Science Photo Library, b Reinhard
Krause/Reuters/Corbis; 10 James Leynse/Corbis; 11t Makoto
Iwafuji/Master Photo Syndication/Sygma/Corbis, b Peter Arnold,
Inc./Alamy; 12 Roger Ressmeyer/Corbis; 13t H. David Seawell/
Corbis, b Kay Nietfeld/epa/Corbis; 14 Jim Sugar/Corbis;
15t Jochen Luebke/epa/Corbis, b George Steinmetz/Corbis;
16t Photo Network/Alamy, b WowWee Group Ltd,
www.wowwee.com: 17 Stephen Hird/Reuters/Corbis; 18 Toru
Hanai/Reuters/Corbis; 19l Klaus Hackenberg/Corbis, r Bubbles
Photolibrary/Alamy; 20 Maximilian Stock Ltd/Science Photo
Library; 21 Peter Menzel/Science Photo Library; 22 Roger
Ressmeyer/Corbis; 23 Jan-Peter Kasper/epa/Corbis;
24 Mashimoto Noboru/Corbis Sygma; 25t Digital
Domain/20th Century Fox/Bureau L.A. Collection/Corbis, b
Haruyoshi Yamaguchi/Sygma/Corbis; 26 Dan Vander Zwalm/
Sygma/Corbis; 27t Danita Delimont/Alamy, b Seth Wenig/
Reuters/Corbis; 28 Jim Sugar/Corbis; 29 Kolvenbach/Alamy
Front cover AllOver Photography/Alamy

DAD0040
32010

9 8 7 6 5 4 3 2 1

Contents

Worktime, Playtime

A robot that does a job in a factory, such as putting screws into holes, might not sound exciting. A walking, talking toy puppy that can learn spoken commands such as "stop" and "sit" sounds like much more fun! Robots created for work might look very different from robots for play, but inside they have many similar parts.

Always at Work

Today there are more and more working robots in factories, offices, schools, hospitals, science laboratories, and homes. Usually they carry out simple jobs and tasks that involve some kind of motion or action, such as paint spraying or putting things into boxes. These robots often have an arm or similar moving part to carry out their jobs. Less often, the whole robot moves around, usually on wheels or rollers.

Dozens of car-making robots join parts with welds and screws, fit the pieces together, clean, paint, and polish. They do this on time and without complaining.

Face to face, a small toy robot waits for instructions from its owner. Or perhaps the owner is waiting for the robot to do something.

Ready to Play

Far away from factories and other workplaces, there are robots that do little more than make us smile or entertain us with funny tricks and silly antics. These are toys for playtime and not much more.

There are also robots that fall somewhere between work and play. Being with them is fun, however, they also help us learn—although we might not realize it at the time. These educational robots can teach us new languages, information about different countries, how to care for the natural world, how to look after our pets, and about science and technology—including how robots work!

ROBOT OR NOT?
○ ○ ○

Too Simple

Is a windup, clockwork mouse on wheels a robot? Or a battery-powered toy dog that walks along? Not really. True, these toys have moving parts, like most robots. But unlike many robots, they do not detect what is happening around them, and they cannot see, hear, or feel when they are touched. They cannot make decisions about what to do, nor can they be instructed or programmed by their human masters. They are mechanical toys, not real robots.

Energy Supplies

Most robots are designed to work on their own, without human help. Once a human has shown a factory robot what to do (for example, moving its arm in a certain way), it can usually carry on without us—but only for a time. All robots have particular needs and rely on supplies from us.

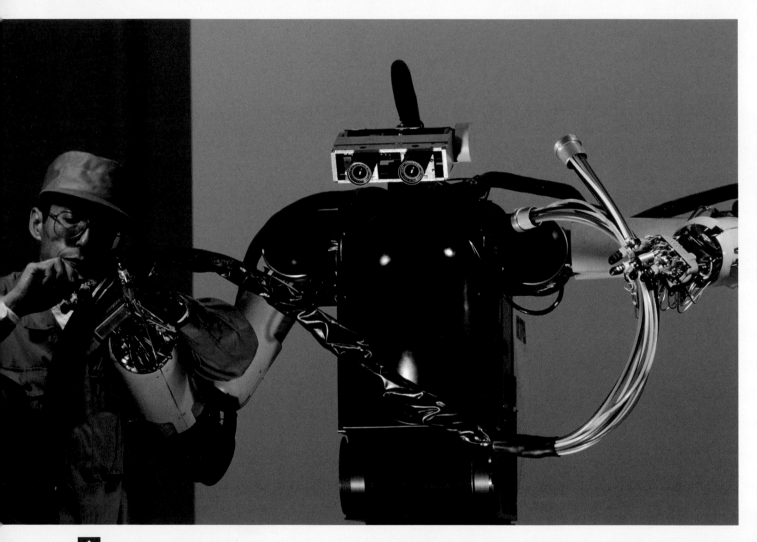

This robot works in part of a nuclear power plant where there could be harmful radiation. Its trainer is safe behind a protective shield and can check the robot's actions.

Hungry for Electricity

Most robots need a supply of electricity. Robot toys work on small, low-power batteries. Big, strong working robots need a more powerful supply of electricity. Usually this is transmitted along cables or wires. Many working robots are fixed in place, to make supplying electricity easier. Mobile working robots such as driverless trucks have big **rechargeable batteries**. Some of these mobile robots rely on humans to plug them into the electrical supply, so they can recharge their batteries. The most advanced robots plug themselves in.

Special Needs

Some robots are **hydraulic**, which means they work by the movement of high-pressure liquid, such as water or oil. This gives them enormous power to cut, bend, and shape materials, even solid metal. Other robots are **pneumatic**, which means they work by the movement of high-pressure air—for example, to blast away dust and dirt. Some need supplies of gas, which they burn to heat objects.

Many robots need supplies of **raw materials**, such as plastic **granules** (small particles) to heat and shape into items or chemicals to mix together to make a product. Something else robots need is a supply of oil to keep them working smoothly or to make the parts they handle fit together easily.

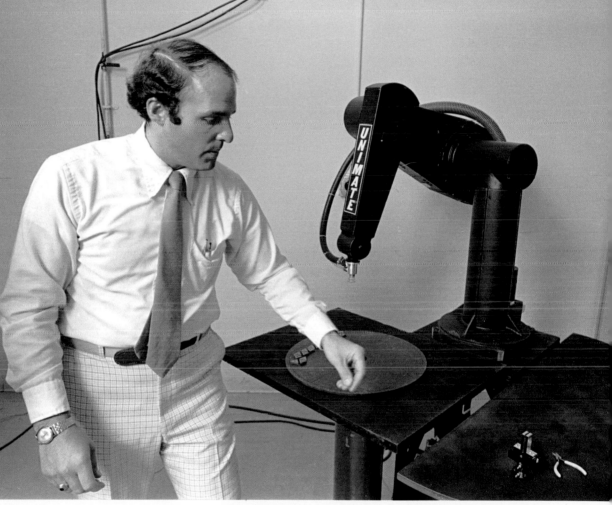

▼ *PUMA the all-purpose robot was first made by Unimate for General Motors. This version from 1980 is showing the jobs it can do.*

ROBOT SUPERSTAR

PUMA

One of the most famous factory robots was PUMA, which stands for Programmable Universal Machine for Assembly. The idea was to make an industrial robot that could do almost any job, given the right instructions. PUMA was developed in the 1970s, and many hundreds were sold. The robot was gradually replaced by more specialized robots.

Robots in Action■

DON'T FORGET!

A common problem for battery-powered robots, especially toy ones, is leaving in the batteries when the robot is not active for a time. Batteries gradually lose their energy and leak their chemicals. This can damage the robot beyond repair.■

Reliable Robo-workers

If you made a list of all the jobs working robots do, it would almost fill this book. Many robots work in factories, industrial centers, warehouses, and manufacturing plants. They push, pull, lift, twist, squeeze, stretch, spray, saw, drill, position, and place all kinds of materials. Robots are the workers that make the products we use every day, from paintbrushes and pencils to computers and cars.

Mass Production

Almost any form of **mass production** (making things in very large quantity) involves robots. Most people have heard of robot welders, sanders, paint sprayers, and polishers for vehicles, as well as robots which fit screws, nuts, bolts, and **rivets**. Stationary manipulator robots stay in one place, and they **manipulate** things. This means they pick up and handle objects, take them apart or put them together, and move them from place to place. Megamanipulators are many times stronger than a person and lift weights of several tons. Micromanipulators handle tiny, delicate parts, such as computer **microchips** far smaller than this letter "o," which our own fingers would fumble with.

▼ *This Titan megamanipulator does not have wheels and is much too heavy for people to move. It is lifted into position by a fork lift.*

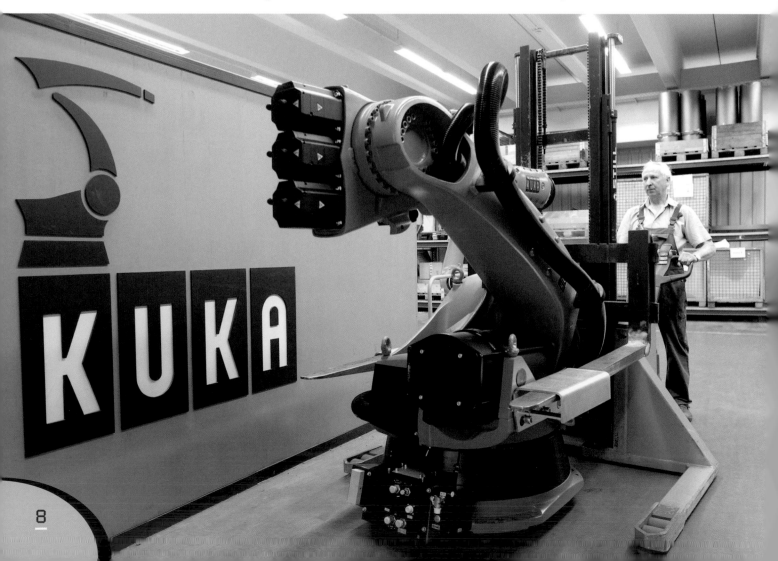

Pickers and Packers

Robot packers lift small objects from a big container or moving **conveyor belt** and place them neatly in boxes. Robot pickers travel along the shelves of giant warehouses, pick up an item here and a product there, and take them to a central point to send out to customers. Robot trucks and carts called **Automated Guided Vehicles (AGVs)** transport things from place to place. They move around factories by following wires in the floor or invisible beams of **infrared light**.

After a robot has been taught or programmed by its human masters, it can do a task exactly the same way, thousands of times, without growing tired or bored.

Da Vinci is a robot surgeon that operates on people. Its tiny mechanical joints can copy many of the movements of a human wrist and hand. Different tips are fitted for various purposes, such as a needle to sew stitches or scissors to cut.

In China, farmer Wu Yulu builds robots as a hobby. This one pulls him along in a rickshaw.

Robots Working at Home

There are always jobs and chores to do at home: cleaning up, washing, ironing, mowing the grass—even cleaning the swimming pool. Now robots can do some of these jobs and give people more free time.

ROBOT SUPERSTAR

Roomba

Robot vacuum cleaner Roomba has been around since 2002. Its contact bumper and infrared beam detect objects so it can find its way around, while it sucks up dust. It then returns to its home base to recharge its batteries. In 2009, Roomba became a member of the Robot Hall of Fame based at the Carnegie Science Center's RoboWorld exhibition in Pittsburgh, Pennsylvania.

Cleaning and Mowing

One of the most boring chores is cleaning. Robot vacuum cleaners can trundle around while people are out, sucking up dust and dirt. They use **sensors** such as contact pads, infrared rays, and **ultrasound beams** to avoid furniture, walls, and stairs. Some types go on what is called a **random walk**, so eventually they cover the entire room. Others have a computer memory and can learn a map of each room they clean.

ROBOT OR NOT?

Robo-dishwasher?

Is a dishwasher a robot? It has moving parts, carries out a task, and we can set its wash cycle, for example, so it does a wash or just a rinse. But a dishwasher does not decide anything for itself, or sense and react to its surroundings. If it could collect dirty dishes from the table and put them away in a cupboard when clean, it would be a real robot!

Guard robots patrol buildings and work sites to check fences, doors, and windows. If they detect intruders, they inform their human controllers at once.

Outside, robo-mowers wander across the lawn on their own. Their sensors detect objects such as trees, rocks, toys, and flower beds, and change direction so that eventually all the grass is mowed. In a similar way, robotic pool cleaners crawl around the walls and bottom of a swimming pool, scrubbing and sucking away the dirt and slime.

Spy-bot

A **webcam** is a camera that sends its pictures to a computer for use over the Internet. Mobile or roving webcams travel around a place and show pictures of what they see while they learn the layouts of the rooms, doorways, and furniture. With an Internet link, these security robots can show you what's happening at your home or workplace while you are away.

Training a Robot

A new robot arrives at a factory ready to start work. What is it going to do? Someone has to teach the robot how to carry out its tasks and then keep an eye on it, in case it "forgets" or makes a mistake.

Computer Programs

There are several ways to give a working robot instructions. One way is to use a computer to program its movements. Imagine that a robot arm's first action is to move its grabber to the right by 30 centimeters to pick up an object. The computer instruction might be: Move 0, 30, 0. That means move up or down zero (nothing), move right 30 centimeters, and move back or forth zero. The next action might be: Move 40, -60, 20, so the grabber goes up 40 centimeters, left 60 centimeters (the minus sign showing left rather than right) and forward 20 centimeters. These numbered positions are known as **coordinates**. A programmer uses sets of coordinates to tell the robot exactly where to move its grabber at every stage.

ROBO-FUTURE

Spoken Instructions

*As computers and **microchips** become faster and more powerful, robots become more advanced—especially at **speech recognition** and understanding what humans say. One day people may be able to instruct working robots simply by talking to them, saying, "Put the object in the box" or "Twist the screw slightly harder."*

▼ *Robo-puppy Aibo was trained to sit and roll over. The operator sent programs to its computer-chip "brain" and spoken commands to its microphone.*

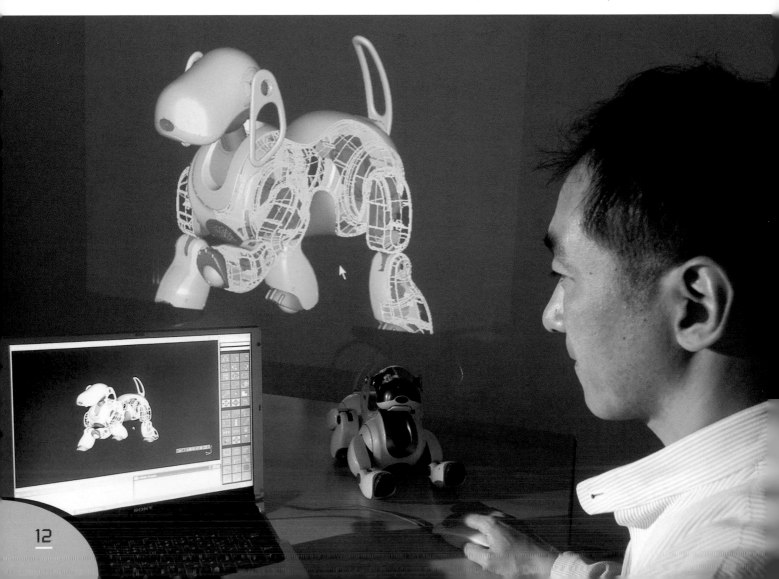

Robots in Action■

KNOW YOUR LIMITS

Active, moving robots need various kinds of built-in safety limits. Their arms, joints, levers, links, and wheels can only move by certain amounts, otherwise they get strained, cracked, and broken. So the motors, pistons, and other parts that power their actions must only move so far, up to a certain limit, to avoid such problems.■

A programmer checks that a robot drill is making holes in exactly the right places.

Do It Like This

Some robots can be taught by moving their parts. First the human teacher puts the robot into instruct or teach mode, ready to receive instructions. Then the teacher holds and moves the robot's arms and other parts in the correct way. Sensors in the arm joints detect how much they move and send the results to the robot's computer memory.

This human-shaped robot has a camera "eye" that detects its teacher's movements, so the robot can copy them.

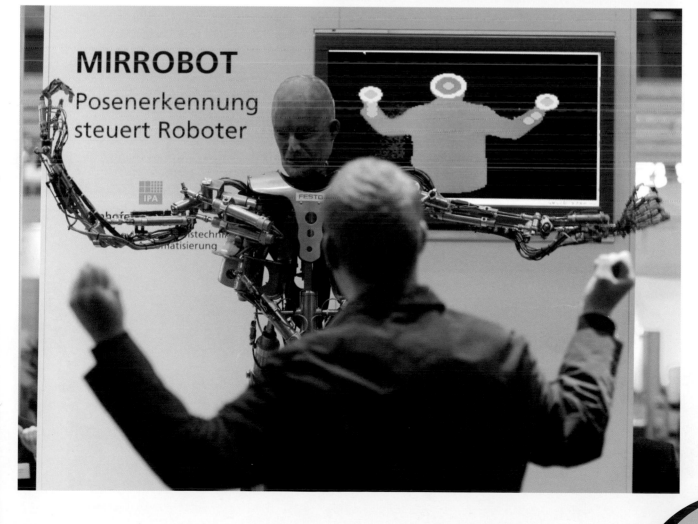

MIRROBOT
Posenerkennung
steuert Roboter

Robot or Human?

How do working robots compare with human workers? There are benefits and drawbacks to both. Which is best depends partly on the task. Some jobs are more suited to robots while others are best done by people.

Robot Plus Points

Robots in factories, warehouses, and similar places can work long hours without ever growing tired or bored. They do not need breaks for drinks, food, or to go to the restroom. They do not lose concentration and forget what they are doing. They do not mind difficult conditions such as heat, cold, odors, and fumes. They do not have holidays or get sick. They can do a task in exactly the same way millions of times. Different robots can be faster, stronger, more precise, or gentler than people—and they do not need to be paid for their work.

Working Conditions

In 2006, the first robotic surgeon operated without human intervention on a 34-year-old man's heart. Observers rated the robot as better than an above-average human surgeon. Designers believe that robots can replace half of all surgeons by 2025.

In a newspaper printing plant, a robot cart delivers huge rolls of paper, giving its human boss time to read and check the paper.

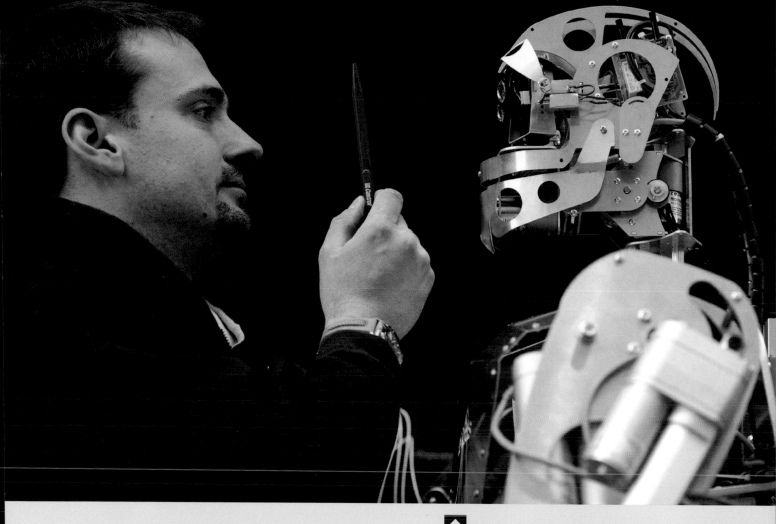

Robot Drawbacks

A robot costs a lot of money to buy and set up. It must be well trained and well maintained. It needs electricity and other supplies, and it cannot work forever. It must be switched off for cleaning and maintenance, which is known as **downtime**. Very occasionally a robot may break down and need to be repaired. All this involves time and money. Also even well-made robots do not last forever; eventually, a factory owner has to spend more money buying new ones.

▲ *Engineers and other experts need to check and adjust their robots and fix them if they break down.*

▼ *Using robots to control traffic means that people do not risk being hit by fast cars. Even so, people need to set them up and take them away.*

Robo-blog■

NEW JOBS FOR OLD

More and more, robots replace people and do the jobs once carried out by human workers. But bringing in lots of robots also makes new kinds of jobs. The robots need designers and engineers to make them, install and train them, as well as check, service, and repair them.■

● It's Playtime!

Toy robots are great fun.
They range from cute animals
to scary ones, from walking
and talking toy robots to
robot cars and planes.
There are even robot
spaceships and aliens.

⏫ *Robot chess players compete against
each other as well as against human players.
They even set out the pieces at the start and
put them away afterwards.*

I obey!

Many toy robots have microphones, which
can detect sounds, such as the words we
speak. A computer inside the robot
compares the sounds with those in its
memory, so it can recognize words such
as stop or go. Then small electric motors
whirr to make the robot move in various
ways. These simple robots are mainly
designed as toys for young children.

⏪ *This radio-controlled
dragonfly is the first robot
toy to take to the skies by
flapping its wings, rather
than using a propeller.*

More expensive robots can do more. Some have cameras or infrared sensors, which detect objects around them, and **pressure pads** or touch bars, which register physical contact. Robots with extra motors have more moving parts and can perform more varied actions. The computer inside can be programmed to make the the robot seem friendly one minute, then frightened the next, or even ready for a fight!

Robot Games

Some robots are designed to play games and do puzzles. There are robots who play chess, checkers, and similar board games. They not only determine the next move in their computer brain, they also have a mechanical arm to lift up the pieces and put them in new positions. Other board games and puzzles have robot characters or playing pieces. You throw dice or take a token, choose your tactics, move your robot forward when possible, save it from disaster, and ideally win the game.

⬇ Robosapien has a similar design to many humanlike robot toys, and the robots in cartoons and movies. It looks menacing and powerful, with big bulging "muscles."

ROBOT SUPERSTAR

Robosapien

The scientific name for all human beings is Homo sapiens. *Robosapien is a human-shaped walking robot, or* **android**. *The first version came out in 2004. The following year, Robosapien V2 was launched, which was bigger, had more features, and a remote control for programming. It could talk, see, hear, learn spoken commands, detect being touched, grip with its hands, walk, bend, lie down, dance, and move in many other ways.*

17

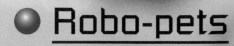 Robo-pets

Many people love pets—dogs, cats, rabbits, rats, guinea pigs, mice, birds, snakes, lizards, fish, spiders, and others. You can buy robot versions of all these animals. These robo-pets are machines rather than living things, but they give their owners a kind of fun and can teach us about real animals.

The i-Dog not only dances, it plays its own music to dance to when you press its nose button.

Digi-pets

Tamagotchis were hugely popular electronic pets during the 1990s, and they are still sold today. These pretend pets are small gadgets with a screen and buttons. The owners must feed, clean, and play with them to keep them well and happy. As Tamagotchis have no moving parts, such as a tail to wag or eyes to blink, they are not really robo-pets. They are usually known as digital pets or virtual pets.

Living Pets

When you own a pet, you have to provide food, drink, and a comfortable place for it to live. You must make sure it is clean and safe, does not get hurt, or suffer illness. Many pets, especially dogs, need exercise and training. This all takes time and usually costs money. The reward is a happy, healthy pet that you can be proud of and which enjoys your company.

▲ A pet such as a guinea pig is a big responsibility. Its owners must buy it food, a cage, bedding, and toys, as well as arrange care if they go on vacation. A robot pet can be turned off!

Just a Machine

Robo-pets have some advantages. You do not have to clean out their cages, take them to the vet if they are ill, or arrange care for them when you go away. They do not smell, make too much noise, or cause problems for people who are allergic to animals. Best of all, you can switch them on and off when you like. After all, they are only machines. Robo-pets can be useful to show people, especially young children, that a pet needs care and attention. Sometimes a robo-pet can act as a trainer, teaching children what it's like to look after a real pet.

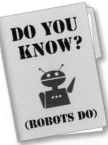

DO YOU KNOW?

(ROBOTS DO)

Bad Owners

It's perhaps a good thing that robot pets cannot talk and send messages to each other. If they could, they might compare their human owners. Some people who are thoughtless and uncaring might gain a reputation as bad pet-owners.

Making a New Robot

Robots, like other machines and devices, are the result of years of work. From first designs, they are tested, redesigned, and tested again, gradually improving all the time. Developing a new robot might take as long as five years!

Computer Designed

Most new robots are designed on computers. In the computer's memory are pictures of essential parts such as levers, motors, joints, gears, and wires. The designers fit these together on the screen in different ways, then see how the parts work together on screen, and how long they might last. For example, a large robot arm must have strong joints. If a slightly weaker joint is used than necessary, the arm might break after a few thousand movements. But, at this stage, this is not important as the robot is still only a design on a computer screen.

ROBOT SUPERSTAR

Unimate

The first real industrial robot was Unimate. In 1961, it began work in a car factory in New Jersey. Unimate was quite simple—a box with a moving arm. Its task was to pick up hot pieces of metal and put them into stacks. The first Unimates were working **prototypes**, *which were tested to see if they would be suitable for factory jobs. They were, and in 1966 they went into mass production. Many robots in today's factories are based on Unimate's original design.*

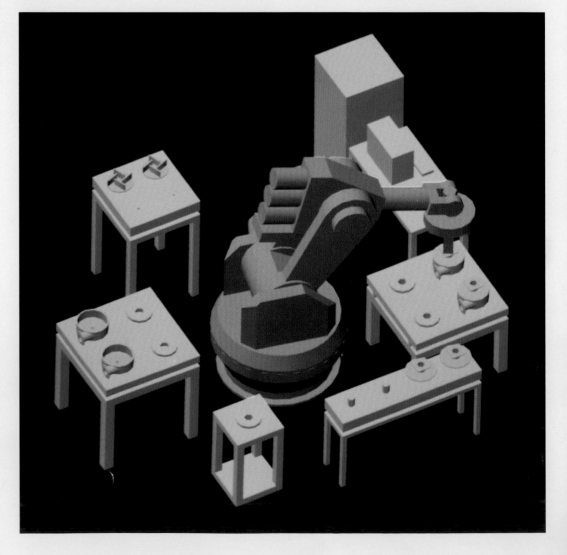

▶▶ *The layout of a factory robot's workplace is designed by a computer, to make sure that the robot can reach all the parts it needs by swinging around and extending its arm.*

Early Stages

After the first design stage, engineers build the robot out of real parts. This is known as a prototype. It is tested to see if it works well and can perform the tasks it has been designed to carry out. When the designers and engineers see the robot as a working machine, they may come up with new ideas for building improved versions.

 A robot designer needs many kinds of tools and equipment, from a sketch pad and pen to first versions of the electric circuits.

Fabb Robots

*A digital **fabricator**, also called a "fabber," can make a three-dimensional solid object automatically from digital data, either by removing material from a block or by adding material layer by layer to form an object. Fabbers can create new parts for testing and assembly into prototype devices, or even low-volume production. In the future, you may be able to "fabb" your own robot at home.*

What Makes a Robot Move?

A robot toy puppy wags its tail. A robot board game player throws dice. A factory robot drills a hole. These are different actions, but in robot design and engineering, they all have the same basis.

Robot Motors

A robot can only carry out actions if it has **actuators**, or devices that cause movement. Usually these are electric motors. A toy mini-robot might have a motor as small as a pea, but the motor in a big industrial robot could be bigger than you. A robot's computer microchips control how long the motor works by sending electricity to it. So when a robot toy animal closes its eyes, the motor switches on long enough to make its eyelids tilt down over its eyes.

Joints for Movement

Human arms and hands are amazingly flexible. That's because we have almost 30 bones and more than 50 joints inside each arm and hand. No robot arm or similar part is so complicated. Robot engineers determine what a robot needs, using the idea of degrees of freedom (DOFs).

A robot arm may have one joint, which moves left or right. This is one DOF. If the engineers add another joint and section, the arm can move up and down, too. That makes two DOFs. A third joint and section allows the arm to move backward and forward, making three DOFs. A swivel or twisting joint allows one section to turn or rotate, making four DOFs. Two more swivel joints bring the total to six DOFs. This is usually all a robot needs and allows the arm to make almost any movement you can imagine.

▼ *Hero 1 shows the range of movement of its claw "fingers." Its "wrist" has one degree of freedom, swiveling up and down. Both are powered by electric motors in round cases.*

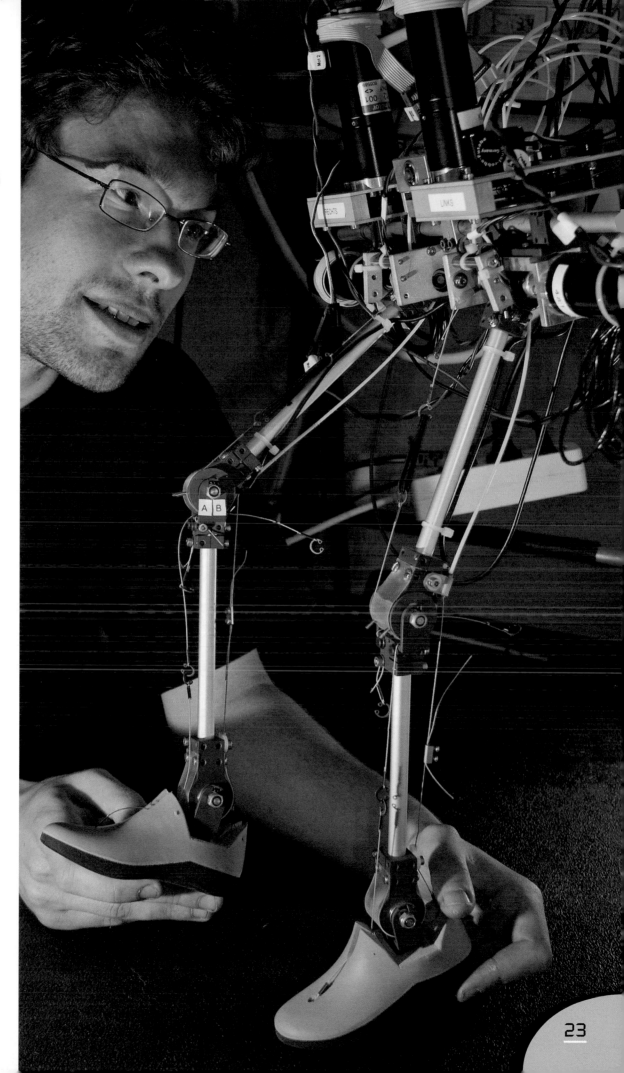

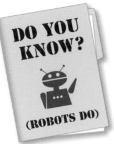
All-important Timing

The timing of a robot's movements is very important. If the eyes on a toy robot close and then open again quickly, the toy seems to blink. If only one eye closes and opens, it winks. If the eyes stay closed for a time, it seems to be asleep. The timing is programmed into the robot's microchip memory. A robot can only perform actions that it is programmed to do.

▶▶ *The JenaWalker series of robots tests various kinds of joints, motors, and controllers. One aim is to help design better artificial hips, knees, feet, and entire legs for disabled people.*

The Robot Business

Not all robots are made and sold in large numbers. Some fail to sell and end up on the scrap heap. Others are produced in small quantities and may become famous, rare, and valuable. Whether a robot is designed for work or play, it's part of the robot business.

Robots for Research

Some robots are one-offs, or part of a limited series, one version after another. They are built to show the skills of their designers and engineers. Often they are called research platforms for trying out new ideas and technology that may help in the future. Only by building and trying out a robot can the designers and engineers make progress.

Mass Production

Other robots are intended solely for mass production and sale, to make money for a company. This is just like any other kind of business. The more that sell, the higher the profit—but it's always a balancing act. A toy robot with advanced features might be fun to

Many big cities have robot stores where people can buy ready-made robots, robot kits, and different parts to make their own designs.

play with, but if it costs thousands of dollars, very few people will be able to afford to buy one, so sales may be low. Manufacturers have to decide on a suitable price for every new robot. This needs to be low enough for people to afford but high enough enough for the makers to make a profit rather than a loss. As well as the manufacturing cost, the makers must pay for advertising and launching a new product. The robo-business is big business.

Not a Bot

Many books, films, and stories feature robot characters. Some are friendly and good, others are nasty and deadly. Sometimes robot makers produce a toy version of each character to play with. However, often this is not a real robot, just a plastic toy with movable parts.

In the 2004 movie I, Robot, Sonny is an advanced robot who helps humans against evil robots. Various toys, models, and games feature the robots from this movie.

ROBOT SUPERSTAR

Aibo

Robot puppy Aibo was introduced in 1999. Later several improved versions were launched, with cameras, microphones, motors, a face with light patterns to show Aibo's mood, a computer "brain" to learn and react, and a memory stick to program new actions and behavior. But the robot world moves on. After 2006, Aibos were no longer manufactured.

Robots and Risks

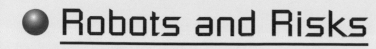

Robots, like other machines and devices, can cause problems. They may break down at an important time. Or parts could fall off and injure people. Working robots with powerful electrical supplies, high-pressure liquids or gases, strong chemicals, and very fast-moving parts are all dangerous if they go haywire.

No Harm to Humans

The three laws of robotics are rules that all robots should obey. They were not written by real robot experts but by **science fiction** storyteller Isaac Asimov, in 1942. The first law says that a robot should not injure a human being or allow a human being to come to harm. In real life, human injuries due to robots do occur, but they are accidents, rather than robots deliberately harming people. In 1979 a man was hit by a robot arm at a factory in Michigan. This was the first recorded human death involving a robot.

▼ *Many factory and warehouse robots, like these in a car factory, are big, strong, and fast. Despite safety equipment, rules and precautions, accidents do happen, but they are very rare.*

◀◀ *Hard hats, face visors, gloves, and tough clothes are all designed to reduce the risk of injury, not only from robots but from any machinery.*

Big Trouble

In factories and on industrial sites, robots work alongside many other big, powerful machines, such as drills and **welding** equipment. All of these can cause harm if they break, so there are many safety features for the machines. Robots are usually designed to stop at once and turn themselves off if there is a breakdown or other problem. Some accidents are caused by people who forget safety advice, rather than the robots.

Small Problems

Small parts can come away from or break off toy robots and leave sharp edges, or they may be swallowed by young children. But these are risks with any playthings, from cuddly teddy bears to model spaceships, not just with robot toys. All these items undergo many tests before they can be sold in stores.

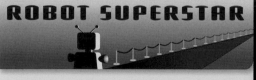

ROBOT SUPERSTAR

Roboraptor

The robot dinosaur Roboraptor has many features, including different moods. If you touch it when it's in a playful mood, it wags its tail, but touch it when it is in guard mood, and it tries to bite! Of course Roboraptor cannot bite hard enough to hurt. But it is one of the first robot toys designed to be scary rather than cute, and it can frighten small children.

What's in Store?

Every year robots become faster and more advanced, with more sensors, actions, and features. Working robots become more reliable, while robots for play offer more extras for less money. The future looks good for our robotic helpers and playthings.

Modern entertainment is multimedia. Humans, robots, models, animatronics, puppets, cartoons, and computer graphics all combine for a feast of fun.

Pleo

Playtime robot Pleo is modeled on a young Camarasaurus dinosaur. It has many sensors, movements, and responses, and it can grow up and learn to react to its owner. Pleo owners can join a club, chat through the Internet, and compare their pets.

Robots in Action▮

ONLINE INFORMATION

Many modern robots are linked through their computers directly to the Internet, without a person being involved. For example, a big working robot can measure the amount of electricity it uses with its electrical sensors and send this information to its control web site. If the robot is using too much electricity, this might mean that some of its motors, bearings, or other parts are getting worn and stiff. So it's time for service.▮

Fluid Movers

As technology improves, play robots become more realistic—especially in their movements. The science of how humans and animals move around is known as **biomechanics**. It is applied to toy animal robots to make their actions more lifelike, so the movements they make are fluid, which means smoother and more natural than the mechanical jerks of old robots. This is done by carefully controlling the motors that cause the movements. The motors speed up and slow down gradually, rather than switching on at full speed right away.

Going Online

Progress in computers and electronics helps robot brains become more powerful, so they can learn faster and have bigger memories. The latest toy robots and their human owners are linked through the Internet into an online community. This trend will grow in the future. Working robots and their human teachers are able to contact each other through the Internet. Online clubs and communities allow people to compare robot features, share advice, and exchange programs for their robots.

Glossary

actuator
A device that produces controlled movements or actions, such as an electric motor, a lever worked by hydraulics, or a piston moved by pneumatics.

AGV
Stands for automated guided vehicle: a truck, cart, or carrier that goes from place to place automatically. AGV can also mean a vehicle that can control itself and work without human help.

android
A robot or similar machine designed to resemble a human body, usually with a face, body, arms, and legs.

biomechanics
The science of how humans and animals move around, including how the bones of the skeleton are pulled by different muscles and how the joints twist and turn.

conveyor belt
A loop-shaped endless belt or a series of rollers that carries items from one place to another, especially in a factory or warehouse.

coordinates
Numbers and/or letters that describe a particular place, such as a point on a map, or a movement such as lifting the arm by a certain amount expressed as a number.

downtime
The time when a robot, computer, or other machine is not working, usually because it is being serviced or repaired, or perhaps because it has broken down.

fabricator
A machine that puts together, assembles, and shapes various parts into a whole finished item or product.

granules
Small lumps or pieces, such as crumbs or grains.

hydraulic
When a liquid under pressure, such as oil or water, is pumped into a pipe to create a pushing force at the other end.

infrared light
Light with waves slightly longer than red light waves, which our eyes cannot see, but which some animals' eyes can.

manipulate
To handle or hold something carefully, moving it or its parts precisely.

mass production
To make a product or item in a very large quantity, usually in a factory using many machines, including robots.

microchip
A small, flat piece of a substance such as silicon, with thousands of microscopic electronic parts on its surface.

pneumatic
When air or a gas under pressure is pumped into a pipe to create a pushing force at the other end.

pressure pads
Small pads with switches inside that detect pressure or touch and produce electrical signals.

prototype
The first version of a machine such as a robot, car, or computer, made to test how it works, find any problems, and see how it can be improved.

random walk
Walking around in a random way, turning to head in different directions at different times, with no plan and no definite place to go.

raw materials
Unshaped substances such as wood, paper, metal, glass, plastic, and various chemicals that are mixed, shaped, molded, and made into specialized parts, which are then fitted together or assembled into a finished item or product.

rechargeable batteries
Electrical batteries (electrical cells) that can have their energy recharged many times by being plugged into another electrical source.

rivets
Metal pins like small, short nails which are used to attach things together. The pins are pushed through lined-up holes in parts that are next to each other. Then their ends are flattened, to hold the parts together very strongly.

science fiction
Made-up stories—fiction—that are based on scientific ideas, equipment, or processes that do not exist yet, but might be possible one day.

sensors
Devices that detect something, such as light, sound, touch, heat, or certain chemicals.

speech recognition
The way a robot or other machine recognizes and identifies the meaning of spoken words or other sounds.

ultrasound beams
Sound waves that are very high pitched or shrill, which our ears cannot hear, but which some animals' ears can.

webcam
A camera linked to a computer and the Internet (World Wide Web), so its pictures can be sent almost anywhere at any time.

welding
Fixing together objects, usually metal or plastic, by heating parts of them. The parts become soft and flow together, then cool and get hard again to give a very strong join.

Further Reading

Ferrari, Mario. *Building Robots with LEGO Mindstorms NXT.* Rockland: Syngress, 2007.

Gifford, Clive. *Robots.* New York: Atheneum, 2008

Hyland, Tony. *Robots at Work and Play.* North Mankato: Smart Apple Media, 2008.

Piddock, Charles. *Future Tech: From Personal Robots to Motorized Monocycles.* Washington, D.C.: National Geographic, 2009.

Strom, Laura Layton. *From Bugbots to Humanoids: Robotics.* New York : Children's Press, 2008.

Web Sites

Lego Mindstorms NXT
Learn how to build your own robot with a Lego Mindstorms robotic kit and talk to robotic experts.
http://mindstorms.lego.com

RoboGames
RoboGames site for U.S. games where the best minds from around the world compete in over 70 different events. Combat robots, walking humanoids, soccer bots, sumo bots, and even androids that do kung fu. Some robots are autonomous, some are remote controlled.
www.robogames.net

Robot Video Clips
Robot Video Clips shows video clips of all kinds of robots in action.
www.robotclips.com

Robot World News
Robot World News covers the top news stories on robotics, artificial intelligence, and related areas, plus fun information on robots such as toys.
www.robotworldnews.com

 Index